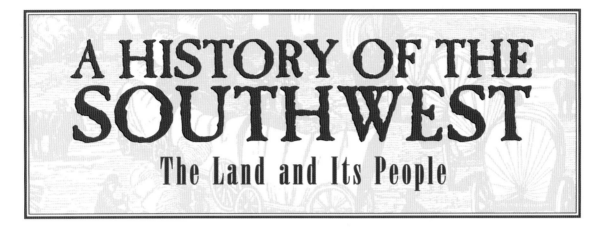

A HISTORY OF THE SOUTHWEST
The Land and Its People

THOMAS E. SHERIDAN

WESTERN NATIONAL PARKS ASSOCIATION

TUCSON, ARIZONA

Sheridan, Thomas E.
    A history of the Southwest : the land and its people / Thomas E. Sheridan.
    p. cm.
    Includes bibliographical reference (p. 78).
    ISBN 1-877856-76-2
    1. Southwest, New–History. I. Title.
F786.S554   1998
979–dc21   97–40075
                                 CIP

Written by Thomas Sheridan
Edited by Derek Gallagher
Designed by Julie Sullivan, Sullivan Scully Design Group
Archival picture research by Jessica Lundburg, Sullivan Scully Design Group
Map by PJ Nidecker, Sullivan Scully Design Group

Prepress color preparation by Graphic Systems
Printing by Four-Colour Imports
Printed in China

OPPOSITE: TOP TO BOTTOM:

PICTOGRAPHS ON INSCRIPTION ROCK

CIVIL WAR REVOLVER

ED SCHIEFFELIN

SANTE FE TRAIN

MEXICAN SPUR

Contents

Prelude

Perhaps because the geologic bones of the Southwest are so visible, the most majestic examples of the natural landscape—the Grand Canyon, Monument Valley, the Sangre de Cristo Mountains—convey a sense of timelessness. Even the cultural symbols—El Morro with its inscriptions carved in sandstone or Betatakin clinging to a cliff in Tsegi Canyon—appear eternal. Our lives change so rapidly we crave even the illusion of permanence.

But human society in the Southwest has always been dynamic and impermanent. During the last five hundred years, Southwestern history has moved through three phases—Incorporation, Extraction, and Transformation—that mark its increasing integration into the global economy. Beginning in the 1500s, Spaniards, Mexicans, and Anglo Americans attempted to incorporate the region, and the Indian peoples who lived there, into their empires or nation-states. All of those peoples—O'odham, River Yumans, Pais, Hopis, Zunis, Ácomas, and Rio Grande Pueblos—resisted incorporation at one time or another.

INSCRIPTION ROCK

OPPOSITE: EL MORRO, NEW MEXICO

Cowboys of African, Anglo, Hispanic, and Indian heritage

Opposite: The prehistoric Puebloan dwellings of Betatakin, Navajo National Monument, Arizona

And other newcomers moving into the region from the north— the Athapaskans who became the Navajos and the Western, Chiricahua, Jicarilla, and Mescalero Apaches—resisted as well, particularly after Old World horses turned them into mounted raiders. Not until Geronimo surrendered for the final time in 1886 was the United States able to establish uncontested political control over the region and bring the era of Incorporation to an end.

The military conquest of the Indians allowed the era of Extraction to begin. From the 1880s until World War II, the economies of Arizona and New Mexico were dominated by extractive industries—stockraising, mining, and agriculture—which converted natural resources such as grasses or copper ores into commodities that were shipped elsewhere for processing and consumption. The Southwest became an extractive colony of the industrial world, linked by its two transcontinental railroads to sources of power and capital outside the region.

Beginning in the late 19th century, however, a few people started to see the Southwest as more than a bundle of resources to be ripped from the ground. Lungers came to Arizona and New Mexico to cure their tuberculosis in the dry desert air. Tourists rode the Santa Fe and Southern Pacific railroads to marvel at the Grand Canyon or to play cowhand on dude ranches in the Sonoran Desert. Presidents like Theodore Roosevelt set aside vast tracts of public domain as national forests, parks, or monuments. Those seeds of Transformation sprouted and flourished during World War II and the postwar boom, when the Southwest became an overwhelming urban society where most people made their living in the manufacturing or service sectors.

Incorporation

This book begins in 1846, three centuries after Francisco Vásquez de Coronado and his conquistadores forced themselves upon the Pueblo peoples of northern New Mexico and encountered the Athapaskan-speaking Querechos traveling by dog train on the Southern Plains. During the era of Incorporation, three major cultures from outside the region converged upon the Southwest. Athapaskans moving southward from Canada collided with Spaniards moving north from central Mexico. Then, after the Louisiana Purchase of 1803, Missouri merchants, Tennessee pioneers, and Irish and German immigrants pushed westward, challenging everyone else for political, economic, and cultural hegemony. This collision of cultures was not always violent—people traded, married, and exchanged ideas with one another as well—but it was first a struggle for power. The Southwest in 1846 was a frontier in the most basic sense of the term—contested ground where no single political entity held uncontested sway. When Mexico and the United States drew lines on the map and went to war, those lines ran through landscapes that bore Tanoan, Keresan, Zunian, Uto-Aztecan, Yuman, and Athapaskan names.

CHRISTMAS LUMINARIOS AT TUMACACORI NATIONAL HISTORICAL PARK, ARIZONA

OPPOSITE: PONDEROSA PINE ON CEBOLLITA MESA, EL MALPAIS NATIONAL MONUMENT, NEW MEXICO

U.S.-MEXICAN WAR

There was enormous arrogance to the conflict on both sides. The Republic of Mexico, a young nation with ancient roots, claimed a vast swath of North America running from the Gulf of Mexico to the Pacific Ocean. Comprising the Mexican territories of New Mexico and Alta California and breakaway Texas, the northern part of the state of Coahuila y Tejas, the region encompassed all of the present U.S. states of Texas, New Mexico, Arizona, Utah, Nevada, and California and portions of Kansas, Colorado, and Wyoming. Yet Mexican settlement in 1846 was restricted to a few strips and pockets in this dry and broken landscape. The rest belonged to Comanches, Apaches, Navajos, Utes, Hopis, Pueblos, O'odham, River Yumans, Pais, Paiutes, and a multitude of California groups.

The United States recognized these claims when it signed the Adams-Onís Treaty of 1819. In return for the establishment of a firm boundary between the Louisiana Purchase and Spanish North America, Spain ceded Florida to the United States two years before Mexico won its independence in 1821. But the relentless westward expansion of settlers from the United States of America soon infringed upon territory claimed by Los Estados Unidos Mexicanos. Anglo Americans wrenched Texas away in 1836. Nine years later, the United States annexed the Lone Star Republic after bitter debate between Northern and Southern interests. Mexico protested, and both nations prepared for war.

PHACELIA AND DESERT AGAVE

COLORADO

San Juan River

UTE

H

CANYON
DE CHELLY

AI

NAVAJO

HOPI

H Fort Defiance

Rio Grande

Taos Pueblo •

Santa
Fe

Jémez Pueblo •

Santo Domingo
Pueblo

Ácoma Pueblo • • Albuquerque

Zuni Pueblo •

JA

PUEBLO

SANGRE DE CRISTO MOUNTAINS

Mountain Branch of Santa Fe Trail

Cimarron Branch of Santa Fe Trail

OKLAHOMA

JICARILLA
APACHE

H Fort Union

NEW MEXICO

H Bosque
Redondo

TEXAS

Pecos River

Fort
Apache

River

H WESTERN
APACHE

Miami

Clifton-Morenci

Rio Ruidoso

Rio Hondo

Lincoln

MESCALERO
APACHE

Goodnight Loving Trail

San Pedro River

Fort
Bowie

icson

N

CHIRICAHUA
APACHE

PURCHASE

Las Cruces •
• Mesilla

Butterfield Trail

Fort
Huachuca

Bisbee

• El Paso

Rio Grande

NORA

CHIHUAHUA

MEXICO

LEGEND

• Town

Mine

H Fort

Indian Territory

Wagon or Cattle Trail

Political Boundary

This was the era of Manifest Destiny, when everyone from politicians like President James Polk to intellectuals like Ralph Waldo Emerson believed that it was America's **"destiny to overspread the whole North American continent with an immense democratic population,"** as newspaper editor John Sullivan proclaimed. The Mexican War was more controversial, but few Americans questioned the nation's need to thwart British interests in Oregon and push westward to the Pacific coast. Once war broke out, then, California became the primary goal of the United States.

GENERAL STEPHEN WATTS KEARNY

BELOW: BENT'S OLD FORT NATIONAL HISTORIC SITE, COLORADO

OPPOSITE: WAGON RUTS STILL MARK THE SANTA FE TRAIL

To secure overland routes to California, however, the United States had to seize New Mexico. Missouri traders eagerly supported annexation in order to control the Santa Fe Trail, which William Becknell had pioneered in 1821. Young Albert Pike may have called

New Mexico the "Siberia of the Mexican Republic" when he visited there in 1833, but for more than two decades, Anglo and Mexican entrepreneurs had braved the Great American Desert to haul merchandise in wagon caravans between Missouri and Santa Fe and reap huge profits. Between 1828 and 1843, the value of U.S. goods entering Mexico through Santa Fe averaged $145,000 a year, while some years, $200,000 of silver rolled across the Southern Plains in the other direction. When General Stephen Watts Kearny assembled his Army of the West in 1846, he followed the deep wagon ruts of the trail from Fort Leavenworth to Bent's Fort in southeastern Colorado. Then he led his 1,600 troops south through Raton Pass to New Mexico's capital, which surrendered on August 18.

NEW MEXICO

Santa Fe in 1846 was a kaleidoscope of contradictions—an isolated outpost on Mexico's far northern frontier that was also a cosmopolitan entrepôt where the Southwest met the Rocky Mountains and the Great Plains. There New Mexicans, Chihuahuans, Anglo Americans, Pueblo Indians, and even Comanches mingled to trade and exchange information about a world beyond that was rapidly closing in around them. Foreign traders and mountain men like Charles Beaubien, Charles Bent, and Cerán St. Vrain married Hispanic women and acquired large tracts of land in northern New Mexico and southern Colorado. Santa Fe and the surrounding Hispanic communities of the upper Rio Grande had survived on the edge of empire for two and a half centuries. Now an army of occupation marched through the dusty streets.

At first, relations were cordial. Kearny proclaimed, **"Not a pepper, not an onion, shall be taken by my troops without pay.** I will protect you in your persons and property and in your religion. Some of your priests have told you that we would ill-treat your women and brand them on the cheek, as you do your mules on the hip, but it is all false." The general even attended mass on Sundays to show his respect for the Catholic populace. But after Kearny departed for California with most of his troops, Colonel Alexander Doniphan's Missouri volunteers drank and brawled, affronting Hispanic honor. Hispanics and Pueblo Indians plotted an insurrection. Several leaders were arrested, but an angry group of rebels in Taos confronted Governor Charles Bent and supposedly told him, "We want your head, gringo, we do not want for any of you gringos to govern us, as we have come to kill you." Then they shot him with arrows and decapitated him.

The revolt was suppressed after U.S. forces battered the pueblo of Taos with artillery, blowing a hole in the adobe mission church and killing about fifty of the rebels. Wary coexistence replaced resistance and bloodshed. Nonetheless, resentment smoldered. Article IX of the Treaty of Guadalupe-Hidalgo, which ended the Mexican War in 1848, assured residents that they would be "maintained and protected in the free enjoyment of their liberty and property, and secured in the free exercise of their religion." But only "free white male inhabitants," including Hispanics but not including

TOP: EARLY WESTERN ENTRE-
PRENEUR CHARLES BENT

ABOVE: MANY ANGLOS
MARRIED HISPANIC WOMEN.
Left to right: HIRAM STEVENS,
PETRA SANTA CRUZ DE
STEVENS, SAM HUGHES,
ATANACIA SANTA CRUZ DE
HUGHES

Indians or African-Americans, were recognized as citizens of the new U.S. territory of New Mexico according to the organic act written to govern the territory until it became a state. In the words of historian Richard Griswold del Castillo, "Approximately eight thousand Pueblo Indians who had been Mexican citizens in 1848 were disenfranchised." Indians throughout the United States did not become citizens until 1924, and Indians in both New Mexico and Arizona could not vote in state or county elections until 1948. The U.S. conquest of New Mexico meant wardship, not freedom, for the politically sophisticated agricultural peoples of Taos, Santa Clara, Jémez, Ácoma, and the other pueblos of the upper Rio Grande watershed.

Hispanics also suffered under the new order. Many Anglo Americans considered Mexicans one step above Indians and African-Americans. South Carolina's Senator John Calhoun opposed granting citizenship to the "colored races" of the Southwest and declared, "Ours, sir, is the Government of the white race." Anglo Americans also did not understand or respect many aspects of Hispanic culture, including land tenure.

OLD SAN JÉRONIMO DE TAOS, NEW MEXICO

Under Spain and Mexico, several hundred land grants were awarded to communities as well as private individuals. Within those communal grants, small plots of farmland may have been divided among individual families, but vast tracts of rangeland and timber—undivided and inalienable—belonged to the community itself. There members of the community—*hijos del pueblo*—gathered firewood, collected wild plants, hunted game, and grazed their herds of cattle and sheep.

One such concession was the Las Vegas Grant east of Santa Fe. In 1861, the U.S. Congress confirmed 496,446 acres belonging to the town of Las Vegas, but Anglo American settlers and speculators began to illegitimately purchase tracts of the Las Vegas Grant and many others, fencing off the land and denying access to people who had used its resources all their lives. By the late 1880s, Hispanic residents were so angered and frustrated by the encroachment that they formed a secret society known as the *Gorras Blancas*, or White Caps, because they hid their faces behind white masks. With great popular support, the Gorras Blancas cut fences, tore up railroad ties, and destroyed Anglo ranches. They also distributed *Nuestra Platforma* (Our Platform), which proclaimed, in part, "We want the Las Vegas Grant settled to the benefit of all concerned, and this we hold is the entire community within the Grant. We want no 'land grabbers' or obstructionists of any sort to interfere. We will watch them."

The resistance of the Gorras Blancas was valiant but futile. Between 1891 and 1904, the U.S. Court of Private Land Claims heard suits involving 34,653,340 acres of land. It rejected claims concerning 32,718,354 acres and confirmed claims covering only 1,934,986 acres. Earlier, Congress had confirmed 45 claims encompassing 6,676,831 acres. To many Hispanics in New Mexico, U.S. citizenship meant dispossession of ancestral range and timber lands.

ARIZONA

Such widespread resistance did not erupt in Arizona because the Mexican presence was much more tenuous. As anthropologist James Officer points out, Hispanic Arizona never amounted to more than 1,000 non-Indian people clinging to settlements like Tubac and Tucson in the Santa Cruz Valley compared to perhaps 60,000 Hispanics in New Mexico. Whenever Mexican miners, ranchers, and farmers tried to expand into the San Pedro Valley or the grasslands of southeastern Arizona, the Apaches drove them back.

JAMES GADSDEN

SOUTHERN ARIZONA
GRASSLANDS

The United States also had much less interest in Arizona. During the Mexican War, U.S. forces passed through Tucson on two occasions but never occupied the region. Under the terms of the Treaty of Guadalupe Hidalgo, Arizona south of the Gila River remained part of Mexico until 1854, when the Gadsden Purchase was ratified. Even then, few Anglos settled in what was then the western half of the Territory of New Mexico.

Beginning in 1849, however, about twenty thousand "argonauts" trudged across sections of southern Arizona to cross the Colorado River at Yuma on their way to the California gold fields. Many traversed the Sierra Madre at Guadalupe Pass. Then they headed down the Santa Cruz Valley through Tubac and Tucson and followed the wagon road pioneered by Lieutenant Colonel Philip St. George Cooke and his Mormon Battalion north to the O'odham villages on the Gila River. They were impressed with

the O'odham, who supplied them with wheat flour and other foodstuffs, but the Arizona desert did not enchant them. "What this God-forsaken country was made for," one forty-niner whimpered, "I am at a loss to discover."

Nonetheless, Arizona's possibilities impressed a few of the sojourners. As John Forsyth passed through the San Rafael Valley in southeastern Arizona, he wrote, "For miles in some places it is as smooth as if rolled & the Grama Grass & wild oats form a magnificent meadow the best natural meadow I ever saw & the stream is fringed with large cotton wood." "The whole country abounds in rich gold and silver mines," another observer reported. "But as soon as a town or rancho is built, the Apaches tear it down and kill all the males and carry off all the females."

The Akimel O'odham: Death of a River

When Spanish ranchers and Jesuit missionaries began colonizing northern Sonora and southern Arizona in the late 1600s, they called it the Pimería Alta, or Upper Pima country. Autonomous groups of Piman-speaking O'odham inhabited a vast desert stretching from the Río Concepción–Río Magdalena drainage on the south to the Gila and Salt rivers on the north. The Spaniards called the O'odham who practiced irrigation agriculture along the rivers Pimas and referred to those who lived in the riverless western deserts as Papagos. The O'odham themselves distinguish between the Akimel O'odham, or River People, and the Tohono O'odham, or Desert People.

The Akimel O'odham living along the Gila never were conquered or missionized by the Spaniards. Nonetheless, they became military allies of the Spaniards and the Mexicans in the 200-year-long guerrilla warfare with the Apaches. They also obtained Old World domestic animals such as cattle and horses and Old World cultigens such as wheat from O'odham gathered into missions to the south. Wheat in particular revolutionized Akimel O'odham agriculture because they could plant it during the winter months when frosts would have killed New World crops like corn, beans, and squash. Wheat became so important that some O'odham even began calling the first month of their year in early summer Wheat Harvest Moon instead of Saguaro Harvest Moon.

AKIMEL O'ODHAM POTTERY

BACKGROUND: MID-NINETEENTH CENTURY ILLUSTRATION OF AKIMEL O'ODHAM WOMEN

Wheat also allowed the Akimel O'odham to become Arizona's first agricultural entrepreneurs. Pimas along the Gila fed U.S. troops during the U.S.–Mexican War and the forty-niners who followed. They supplied Butterfield stage coaches in the 1850s and soldiers on both sides of the War Between the States. By 1870, the Akimel O'odham were selling or trading several million pounds of wheat a year and Pima fields served as the breadbasket of the young Arizona Territory. Because of their importance, the U.S. government granted the Akimel O'odham and their Yuman-speaking Maricopa neighbors the first Indian reservation in Arizona in 1859.

Beginning in the late 1860s, however, Anglo and Mexican farmers up the Gila River began digging canals and diverting Pima water. Crops failed. Trees withered. By 1895, the Akimel O'odham were starving, and the government had to issue them rations. When Anglos first entered Arizona, the O'odham had fed the territory. Within a generation of U.S. rule, they could no longer feed themselves.

GILA RIVER, ARIZONA

The Early Indian Wars

*I*ndian resistance was the greatest single obstacle to Hispanic and Anglo settlement in Arizona and New Mexico. During Spanish colonial and Mexican periods, Hispanics in both New Mexico and Arizona forged military alliances with settled agricultural peoples like the Pueblo groups and the O'odham and Maricopas. Other Indian nations waged successful guerrilla warfare against European and Euro-American encroachment. They also developed economies that relied in part on livestock raiding. Uto-Aztecan speaking Utes ran off cattle, sheep, and horses from the communities of northern New Mexico. Comanches, a Shoshonean people who came to dominate the Southern Plains in the eighteenth century, raided and traded from New Mexico to Coahuila. But it was the Athapaskan-speaking Navajos and Western, Chiricahua,

Apache ranchería

Opposite: Mt. Taylor, New Mexico

Mescalero, and Jicarilla Apaches who destroyed any attempt to establish direct connections between New Mexico and Arizona and kept the Southwest a frontier until Geronimo and his small band of Chiricahuas surrendered in 1886.

Many Navajos and Apaches trace their origins to specific sacred places—canyons, caves, or mountain ranges—in the Southwest. Dzil Ligai (11,590-foot Mt. Baldy) in the White Mountains of Arizona is sacred to many Western Apaches, while the Diné Bikeyah (Navajo Country) is bounded by the four sacred peaks of White Shell Mountain (Blanca Peak in central New Mexico) to the east, Blue Bead Mountain (Mount Taylor in northwestern New Mexico) to the south, Abalone Shell Mountain (San Francisco Peak in north central Arizona) to the west, and Obsidian Mountain (Hesperus or La Plata Peak in southwestern Colorado) to the north. Most archaeologists believe that small bands of Athapaskans did not begin to enter the region until the 1300s and 1400s as they made their way south from Canada along the western edge of the Great Plains. By the seventeenth century, some of these groups had moved into the Four Corners area, where they became the Navajos, or Diné.

Others occupied mountain valleys in eastern Arizona and western New Mexico, developing into the Western and Chiricahua Apaches. Still others fought the Comanches for access to the great buffalo herds in Oklahoma and Texas. The Comanches eventually won, driving the Lipan and Mescalero Apaches south and west. Mediated by European guns and Spanish horses, the shifting geopolitics of the Great Plains set the Apaches on a collision course with Spanish settlers in New Mexico, Texas, Chihuahua, Coahuila, Sonora, and Arizona. Anglo pioneers inherited and aggravated that conflict.

During the 1850s, the U.S. government established a series of forts in New Mexico and Arizona, but military campaigns were inconclusive. In Arizona, the Apaches and the U.S. army circled warily around one another but rarely fought. The army and the Navajos, in contrast, swung back and forth between peace and war. When U.S. forces occupied New Mexico in 1846, the Navajos had become the greatest pastoralists in native North America. Like the Apaches, they ran off Hispanic herds. Unlike the Apaches, however, they used those stolen animals to build up their own herds. "It is estimated that the tribe possesses 30,000 head of horned cattle, 500,000 sheep and 10,000 head of horses, mules, and asses," reported Charles Bent, New Mexico's first territorial governor, "it not being a rare instance for one individual to possess 5,000 to 10,000 sheep and 400 to 500 head of other stock." U.S. attempts to stop their raids on the New Mexicans angered the Diné, especially since the soldiers did little to prevent New Mexican slave raids against the Navajos. "This is our war," Navajo leader Zarcillos Largo told Colonel Alexander Doniphan. **"We have more right to complain of your interfering in our war than you have to quarrel with us for continuing a war we had begun long before you got here."**

KIT CARSON'S RIFLE AND TRUNK

RIGHT: APACHE WAR HEADDRESS

In 1862, however, an ambitious martinet–Brigadier General James H. Carleton–marched across Arizona into New Mexico at the head of the California Column of 2,350 Union volunteers. Bitterly disappointed that there were no more Confederates to fight, Carleton turned his self-righteous wrath against the Mescalero Apaches. "All Indian men of that tribe are to be killed whenever and wherever you can find them," he told Christopher "Kit" Carson, the Taos mountain man he chose to carry out his brutal campaign. "If the Indians send in a flag and desire to treat for peace, say to the bearer that when the people of New Mexico were attacked by the Texans, the Mescaleros broke their treaty of peace, and murdered innocent people, and ran off their stock; that now our hands are untied, and you have been sent to punish them for their treachery and their crimes."

Carson refused to carry out Carleton's orders strictly to the letter, but he did coordinate a three-pronged offensive against the Mescaleros in the Sacramento Mountains of southern New Mexico. Imprisoning men as well as women and children at Fort Stanton, Carson sent Chief Cadete and four other Mescaleros to surrender to Carleton in Santa Fe. "Your troops are everywhere; our springs and waterholes are either occupied or overlooked by your young men," Cadete told Carleton. "You have driven us from our last and best stronghold, and we have no more heart. Do with us as may seem good to you, but do not forget we are men and braves."

Carleton responded by shipping the Mescaleros to a cottonwood-lined elbow of the Pecos River known as Bosque Redondo, which Carleton had first visited when he was a brevet major stationed at Fort Union in the 1850s. Then he dispatched Carson against the Navajos. Again, the iron-willed general issued merciless orders. "Say to them, 'Go to the Bosque Redondo, or we will pursue and destroy you. We will not make peace with you on any other terms.'" In July 1863, Carson marched off to Fort Defiance, which he renamed Fort Canby, with 700 soldiers and Ute and Pueblo scouts. The scouts tracked down the Diné, killing the men and keeping the women and children as slaves. The soldiers carried out a scorched-earth campaign, burning cornfields

TOP: GENERAL JAMES CARLETON

ABOVE: CHRISTOPHER 'KIT' CARSON

TOP: NAVAJOS UNDER GUARD AT
THE BOSQUE REDONDO
RESERVATION

CENTER: CHIEF MANUELITO,
ONE OF THE LAST NAVAJO LEAD-
ERS TO SURRENDER IN 1866

OPPOSITE: SPIDER ROCK IN
CANYON DE CHELLY NATIONAL
MONUMENT, ARIZONA

and slaughtering Navajo herds. Then, as summer turned to fall and fall turned into bitter winter, Carson rode into the last Diné stronghold of Canyon de Chelly, where his forces cut down Navajo peach orchards and killed more livestock.

Some Navajos escaped to Black Mesa or the rim of the Grand Canyon, but more than 9,000 of the Diné—sick, starving, freezing—surrendered to Carson. Then they began the Long Walk to Bosque Redondo, which Carleton renamed Fort Sumner. Hundreds died along the trail. "The trip was made on foot," Curly Tso recalled. **"People were shot down on the spot if they complained about being tired or sick, or if they stopped to help someone. There was absolutely no mercy."** Once they reached the reservation, which can only be described as a concentration camp, the Diné were crowded together with 500 Mescaleros. Rations were short. Firewood was scarce. Pecos water was high in alkali. Comanches stole what little property the Mescaleros and Navajos had, and the Mescaleros and Navajos, who were enemies, fought among themselves.

On November 3, 1865, outnumbered by the Navajos and dying from a measles epidemic, the Mescaleros bolted. Some Navajos escaped as well, but the rest remained in exile, where several thousand more of the Diné perished from starvation or diseases like dysentery and smallpox. When the government finally realized in 1868 that Carleton's "experiment" on the Pecos was a cruel failure, only 4,000 Navajos survived to return to their homeland in the Four Corners.

The Civil War in the Southwest

When the Civil War finally broke out in 1861, Arizona and New Mexico became battlegrounds for one old familiar reason: California. Southern interests had dreamed of an all-weather transcontinental railroad linking the South with California gold fields and Pacific coast ports for at least a decade before the Union was sundered. After the Confederacy declared its independence, the territory of New Mexico seemed ripe for the plucking. Most of the officers in the Department of New Mexico joined the South. Southern sympathizers, many of them Texas ranchers like William Oury, dominated Tucson and the Mesilla Valley. Colonel John Baylor quickly recruited 350 Texas Mounted Volunteers, occupied deserted Fort Bliss outside El Paso, and then defeated Union troops fleeing Fort Filmore.

GENERAL H. H. SIBLEY

Flushed with these easy victories, Baylor declared all New Mexico south of the 34th parallel the new Confederate territory of Arizona with its capital in Mesilla.

For a while it seemed the Southwest would fly the Rebel flag. Union forces quickly abandoned Forts Breckenridge and Buchanan in southern Arizona, burning all military supplies they could not carry. In December 1861, West Point–trained General Henry Hopkins Sibley arrived in El Paso with 2,600 more Texans to assume command of all Confederate forces in New Mexico. He sent Captain Sherod Hunter to occupy Tucson and defend his western flanks against Union reinforcements from California. Then he turned north up the Rio Grande to attack Fort Craig, where Colonel Edward Canby had consolidated Union forces. Sibley's Texans beat the Yankees at the bloody Battle of Valverde just north of Fort Craig, but Canby held the fort itself.

MILITARY REVOLVERS FROM THE CIVIL WAR ERA

Sibley made his first major mistake when he left Canby behind and marched north to seize Albuquerque and Santa Fe. Union troops destroyed ammunition and foodstuffs as they retreated to the military depot of Fort Union. Sibley hoped to obtain the supplies he needed from New Mexican settlers, but the largely Hispanic

population in the north did not share the Southern sympathies of New Mexicans in the Mesilla Valley. On the contrary, many of them hated Texans and refused to accept Confederate currency. Sibley's troops grew hungrier and hungrier as they rode north.

That made Fort Union an even more attractive target. But Fort Union had been reinforced by a regiment of Colorado Volunteers, who squared off against the Texans at Glorieta Pass fifteen miles southeast of Santa Fe. Guided by Colonel Manuel Chaves of the New Mexico Volunteers, Major John Chivington sneaked behind the Confederates and destroyed 73 wagons of supplies and bayoneted more than 500 horses and mules. Two years later, Chivington led the massacre of the Cheyennes at Sand Creek, but his actions in Apache Canyon on the west end of Glorieta Pass helped save New Mexico for the Union. Sibley staggered back to Texas and Hunter abandoned Tucson. By the time General Carleton and his California Column crossed the Mojave Desert into Arizona and New Mexico, there were no more Confederates left to fight.

Nonetheless, the Civil War had lasting consequences for the Southwest. On February 20, 1863, President Lincoln signed a bill creating the new territory of Arizona. Unlike Confederate Arizona, however, Union Arizona encompassed the western rather than the southern portions of New Mexico. The reason for the split glittered in the gold from new diggings in the mountains of central Arizona, far to the north of the old Spanish and Mexican settlements of the Santa Cruz Valley. Prescott, an infant town that had sprung up in the middle of this gold rush, became Arizona's first territorial capital. Its architecture and layout—Victorian houses arranged around a courthouse square—attest to its Anglo rather than Hispanic origin.

ABOVE: FORT UNION RUINS, FORT UNION NATIONAL MONUMENT, NEW MEXICO

BACKGROUND: REENACTMENT OF THE BATTLE OF PICACHO PASS

FREIGHTERS AND CONTRACTORS

Soon after Sherod Hunter rode into Tucson on February 28, 1862, he demanded that all Union sympathizers swear an oath of allegiance to the Confederacy. Estevan Ochoa, a Chihuahuan who grew up hauling freight for his brother along the Santa Fe Trail, politely refused. A small, dapper man with a neatly trimmed beard, Ochoa reputedly said, "Captain Hunter, it is out of the question for me to swear allegiance to any party or power hostile to the United States Government; for to that government I owe all my prosperity and happiness. When, Sir, do you wish me to go?"

Hunter allowed Ochoa to ride out of Tucson alone and head east into

TOP: ESTEVAN OCHOA

ABOVE: EARLY FREIGHT WAGONS IN ARIZONA

Chiricahua Apache territory toward Mesilla, where Ochoa's freighting business had been headquartered before he moved to Tucson. No one expected him to reach his destination. But he did, returning to Tucson a few months later after the Confederates had fled.

Ochoa and Pinckney Randolph Tully resumed their partnership in long-distance freighting, hauling goods into Arizona in sixteen-foot-long Murphy wagons from Yuma, Guaymas, and the commercial centers of Missouri. By 1880, Tully, Ochoa, and Company employed hundreds and had developed into one of the largest, most diversified economic endeavors in the Southwest. Tully and Ochoa owned mercantile stores. They bought mining claims. They experimented with sheepraising and wool processing. Ochoa and his partner were true entrepreneurs—risk-takers continually searching for new ways to make money on a risky frontier.

But the foundation of Tully, Ochoa, and Company's business—like all the other freighters and merchants in the Arizona and New Mexico territories—was army contracts. During the 1860s and 1870s, the U.S. army was, in the words of historian Darlis Miller, "the single largest purchasing and employment agency in the Southwest." Soldiers scattered across Arizona and New Mexico had to be fed and supplied. Later, after Indians had been confined to reservations, rations of beef, beans, and flour had to be provided. Southwestern pioneers may have been rugged individuals, but then, as now, their livelihoods depended on the federal government.

The contractors themselves were a diverse lot. Some, like Ochoa and the Aguirre brothers, Epifanio, Pedro, Conrado, and Yjinio, came from northern Mexico, where they had grown up fighting Apaches and cracking whips over mules along the Chihuahua and Santa Fe Trails. Others, like Philip Drachman, Henry Lesinsky, Michael Goldwater, and the Staab brothers, Zadoc and Abraham, were Jews fleeing pogroms in Germany, Poland, and Russia. These immigrants joined Southern cattle ranchers and Northern merchants to gamble their fortunes on the Southwestern frontier.

For a time, in places like Santa Fe, Mesilla, Las Cruces, and Tucson, they created a vital bicultural frontier society. The scale of the early territorial economy was mercantile rather than industrial. Mexican entrepreneurs could compete with Anglo entrepreneurs in flour milling, ranching, and freighting. Moreover, Anglos and Mexicans like Tully and Ochoa became friends and went into business with one another. Anglo men and Mexican women formed more intimate ties. In southern Arizona, many of the most prominent Anglo pioneers–Governor Anson P.K. Safford, Peter Brady, Sam Hughes, Augustus Brichta, and Tully himself–married into Mexican families. In New Mexico, the rate of intermarriage was even greater. According to the 1870 federal census

manuscripts, 90 percent of the Anglo men in Las Cruces who married wed Mexican
wives. Mesilla with 83 percent and Santa Fe with 63 percent followed close behind.
These men undoubtedly internalized aspects of Mexican and Hispanic culture from
their business associates and spouses. Their children were even more Mexicanized.
Some, such as Bernabe Brichta and P. R. Tully's adopted son Carlos, chose to identify
with their Mexican rather than their Anglo heritage despite growing anti-Mexican
racism and discrimination in the region. Early territorial society in the Southwest had
deep Mexican roots.

VIOLENCE IN LINCOLN COUNTY

As more Anglos moved into the Southwest, however, some of the newcomers
wanted to tear up those roots and drive out the "damned greasers." One arena of conflict
was enormous Lincoln County, which sprawled across nearly 30,000 square miles of
southeastern New Mexico. There, small communities of Hispanic farmers and sheep-
raisers encountered ranchers like John Chisum and outlaws one step ahead of the Texas
Rangers. The Texans were moving westward, following the cattle trail blazed by
Charles Goodnight and Oliver Loving up the Pecos River to the gold mines of Colorado.
Hardened by bitter family feuds and the carnage of the Civil War, many of
these Texas cowboys were quick to shoot to defend their honor.
They were even quicker to fire if the targets were
Mexican. The Texas revolt and the Mexican War
had spawned deep contempt and burning hatred between Mexicans
and Texans. As historian
Robert Utley wryly
notes, "New Mexicans
of Spanish descent
and Texans did not
share Lincoln County
comfortably."

OPPOSITE: THE PECOS RIVER IN
NEW MEXICO

TEXAS COWBOYS

One of the worst episodes was the Horrell War, which spread its venom in the winter of 1873–74. Ben Horrell and his four brothers had settled along the Ruidoso River to escape a feud in Lampasas, Texas. On December 1, Horrell and two friends got drunk and shot up the little adobe county seat of Lincoln. Deputy Juan Martínez tried to arrest them. Martínez and one of the Anglos were killed in the gunfire. Enraged, the largely Hispanic populace of Lincoln shot Horrell and the other Anglo.

Three weeks later, the four surviving Horrell brothers and their allies sneaked up to a Hispanic wedding dance and whispered, **"Come on, we'll make them dance to our music."** Blazing away through the windows, they murdered four men and wounded two women and a boy. They continued their bloody rampage by slaughtering five Mexican freighters and killing young Joe Haskins simply because he had a Hispanic wife.

HISTORIC WANTED POSTER

BILLY THE KID

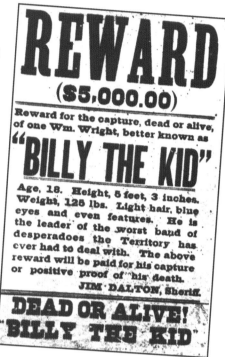

The Horrells finally left Lincoln County and returned to Texas. But more violence was brewing. Rustlers and small stockmen fought Chisum for control of the rich black-grama Pecos Plains. Meanwhile, in the town of Lincoln itself, three Irish immigrants named Lawrence Murphy, James Dolan, and John Riley ran a mercantile establishment known as "The House." They controlled government contracts. They corrupted Indian agents. They drove ranchers and farmers into debt and seized their land. The alcoholic Murphy and his two younger protégés also dominated the Democratic Party and manipulated the courts. With strong ties to the Santa Fe Ring and a band of rustlers and outlaws known as "The Boys," the Irishmen controlled Lincoln County and killed or ran off anyone who challenged them.

Then, early in 1877, a young Englishman named John Tunstall opened a rival store and began forming his own "ring," which included a Scottish lawyer named Alexander McSween, Dick Brewer, a cowboy in debt to The House, and a wiry young drifter who called himself William H. Bonney.

ADOBE BUILDING,
LINCOLN, NEW MEXICO

The opening salvo in the Lincoln County War took place on February 18, 1878, when Tunstall was ambushed and killed. Led by Brewer, Tunstall's supporters dubbed themselves "The Regulators" and a group of them ambushed Sheriff William Brady, a Dolan partisan, on April 1. Three days later, Brewer died in a gunfight at the headquarters of the Mescalero Indian Agency. The violence reached a crescendo during a five-day siege of Alexander McSween's home from July 15 to July 19, when McSween and three of his companions were shot to death while fleeing the burning building.

Dolan, who ran The House after Murphy drank himself to death, had won the war over Lincoln County. But it was a Pyrrhic victory. Dolan's firm went bankrupt. Gold strikes west of Lincoln shifted the economic balance of power and consigned Lincoln itself to the backwaters of Western history. Nonetheless, the violence continued, aimless, parasitic, fueled by whiskey, racial tensions, and the code of the West.

Six groups of bandits operated in Lincoln County after the war ended. One, "The Wrestlers," led by a Texan named John Selman, raped, murdered, and plundered the Hondo, Ruidoso, and Bonito river valleys. Hispanic settlers grew so alarmed that several suggested mounting a war of extermination against the Tejanos before the Tejanos exterminated them.

Meanwhile, William Bonney escaped from the conflagration at McSween's to ride into legend as Billy the Kid. He drifted from cattle rustling to gunfights with no apparent purpose or goal until Sheriff Pat Garrett shot him in the dark at Fort Sumner on July 14, 1881.

The Santa Fe Ring and the Tucson Ring

"Everything in New Mexico that pays at all," John Tunstall wrote to his parents in 1877, the year before his death, "is worked by a 'ring,' there is the 'Indian ring,' the 'army ring,' the 'political ring,' the 'legal ring,' the 'Roman Catholic ring,' the 'cattle ring,' the 'horsethieves ring,' the 'land ring,' and half a dozen other rings; now to make things stick 'to do any good,' it is necessary either to get into a ring or to make one for yourself."

THOMAS BENTON CATRON

BELOW: ESKIMINZIN, THE LEADER OF THE ARAVAIPA APACHE BAND AT THE TIME OF THE CAMP GRANT MASSACRE

OPPOSITE: TUCSON MOUNTAINS, SAGUARO NATIONAL PARK, ARIZONA

BACKGROUND: PEARL STREET IN TERRITORIAL TUCSON

Citizens made cynical by the political corruption of the Grant administration saw rings everywhere. And the biggest ring of all in New Mexico was the so-called "Santa Fe Ring," run by Stephen Benton Elkins and Thomas Benton Catron. Two lawyers from Missouri who became law partners, Elkins and Catron made fortunes speculating in Spanish and Mexican land grants. The first was the Maxwell Land Grant northeast of Taos, which had been given to Guadalupe Miranda and Charles Beaubien in 1841. Beaubien's son-in-law, Lucien Maxwell, acquired the grant and argued that it encompassed nearly two million acres. The U.S. Interior Department contended it included only 97,000 acres. After ten years of litigation, Elkins as territorial delegate made an end-run around the Secretary of the Interior and won confirmation of more than 1.7 million acres of land.

Elkins eventually left New Mexico to become a U.S. senator from West Virginia. Catron, on the other hand, remained in New Mexico, where he put together a shifting alliance of lawyers, newspaper editors, and politicians that wielded enormous political and economic power for half a century. He also acquired interest in seventy-five grants and amassed nearly two million acres of land. But was the Santa Fe Ring a nefarious reality? "No one has documented its membership, organization, techniques, and purposes to show that it existed as an entity rather than simply as a group of men individually pursuing similar ends in similar ways," observes historian Robert Utley.

The same warning needs to be issued about the "Tucson Ring," which supposedly included all the major Tucson merchants supplying army posts in Arizona. The Tucson Ring has been accused of colluding with territorial officials to win army contracts and of masterminding the Camp Grant Massacre, where more than 100 Aravaipa Apaches were ambushed and slain. But after carefully studying army contracts in the Southwest, historian Darlis Miller concluded, "Fraud was not rampant—a dishonest contractor was the exception rather than the rule." Nonetheless, the reality of this shadowy cabal has become unquestioned dogma in Arizona history. As historian C. L. Sonnichsen remarked, **". . . the myth of the Tucson Ring is so commonly accepted that many a popular novelist would have trouble plotting his stories if he were deprived of the wicked ring as a whipping boy."**

THE MILITARY CONQUEST OF THE INDIANS

*B*loodshed begets bloodshed, and the Southwestern frontier was a place where, in the words of Latin American historians Silvio Duncan Baretta and John Markoff, no one had "an enduring monopoly on violence." By the 1870s, however, the frontier was closing in around the Comanches and Apaches. While governor of Spanish New Mexico, Juan Bautista de Anza had forged an enduring peace between the Comanches and New Mexicans in 1786, but treaties between the Texans and Comanches never lasted very long. Even though the Medicine Lodge treaty of 1867 set aside nearly three million acres in southwestern Oklahoma for the Comanches, Ten Bears, a chief of the Yamparika band, expressed the sentiments of many when he said, **"I was born upon the prairie, where the wind blew free and there was nothing to break the light of the sun.** I was born where there were no enclosures and everything drew a free breath. I want to die there and not within walls. I know every stream and every wood between the Rio Grande and the Arkansas. I have hunted and lived over that country. I live like my fathers before me and like them I lived happily." Many Comanches refused to confine themselves to the reservation, and in 1874 and 1875, U.S. troops converged on the Texas Panhandle from posts in Kansas, Texas, and New Mexico, including Fort Union.

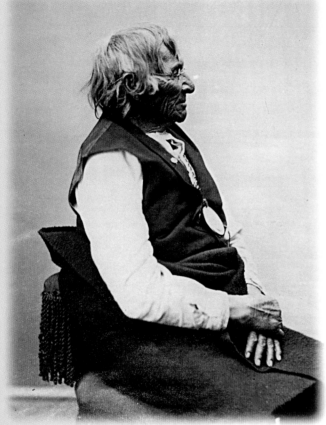

TEN BEARS

OPPOSITE: BOULDER CREEK, BATTLESHIP MOUNTAIN, SUPERSTITION WILDERNESS AREA, TONTO NATIONAL FOREST, ARIZONA

Few Comanche warriors died during the campaigns, but the soldiers destroyed their supplies and their mobility. In one attack on Palo Duro Canyon, 1,424 Comanche horses were seized and more than 1,000 were slaughtered. By summer 1875, all but a handful of Comanches had surrendered. The last Comanche raid took place at a ranch south of Big Spring, Texas, in 1879.

General George Crook defeated the Western Apaches and Yuman-speaking Yavapais in central Arizona during the 1870s as well. In the fall of 1872, nine columns of soldiers scoured the rugged homelands of the Indians from the San Francisco Peaks on the north to the Superstition Mountains on the south. "The officers and men worked day and

night," Crook observed in his 1873 annual report, "and with our Indian allies would crawl upon their hands and knees for long distances over terrible canyons and precipices where the slightest mishap would have resulted in instant death, in order that when daylight came they might attack their enemy and secure the advantage of surprise." Major battles were rare; one exception was Skeleton Cave in the Salt River Canyon, where soldiers killed seventy-six Yavapais from the Kewevkapaya group who had taken refuge in the rock shelter. More devastating was the destruction of Indian weapons and stored food. After Crook's relentless winter campaign, most Yavapais and Western Apaches surrendered. The general reported that Delshay, a Tonto Apache chief, had told him that "now the very rocks had gotten soft, they couldn't put their foot anywhere without leaving an impression by which we could follow."

At first, the Yavapais and Apaches were confined to small reservations near their territories. In 1874, however, the government decided to place all the Indians on the San Carlos division of the giant White Mountain Reservation north of the Gila River in order to control and supply them with rations more easily. The first group to be transferred were Yavapais and Western Apaches from Camps Verde and Date Creek. For eight days in late February and early March 1875, they trudged at gunpoint across central Arizona's broken terrain, leaving behind the sacred landscapes of their people. More than 100 died. The rest, once they reached San Carlos, lived in spiritual as well as physical exile on the bleak creosote flats near the Indian agency, where everything from food to firewood had to be rationed. **"It was an outrageous proceeding,"** wrote Crook's aide-de-camp John Bourke, **"one for which I would still blush had I not long since gotten over blushing for anything that the United States Government did in Indian matters."**

GENERAL CROOK RELIED HEAVILY ON INDIAN SCOUTS

OPPOSITE: WEAVER'S NEEDLE IN THE SUPERSTITION MOUNTAINS, ARIZONA

The government also tried to resettle the Chiricahua Apaches at San Carlos. But the Chiricahuas, straddling Mexico and the United States, had not yet been broken to the new order. In 1872, Cochise, chief of the Chokonen band, even negotiated with Crook's predecessor, General O. O. Howard, for a reservation in southeastern Arizona running from the Dragoon Mountains on the west to the Peloncillos on the east. The reservation disintegrated after Cochise's death in 1874. Three years later, 453 Chiricahuas under Geronimo and Victorio yielded to reservation life, but most of them fled three months later. Victorio and his band of Chihenne Chiricahuas returned to their homeland of Ojo Caliente in western New Mexico, living peacefully until the government tried to force them to return to San Carlos, which they had grown to despise.

In 1879, Victorio realized that U.S. authorities were never going to allow the Chihennes to remain in the Mogollons, the Blacks, and the other mountains they loved. So he gathered Chiricahuas, Mescaleros, and even a few Comanches and led his band on one of the most astounding guerrilla campaigns in the history of the continent. For more than a year, Apache men, women, and children outfoxed, outfought, and outran thousands of U.S. troops in Arizona and New Mexico. But as they moved eastward, African-American cavalrymen from New Mexico and west Texas hounded the travel-weary Apache families. Victorio may have been headed for the Bolsón de Mapimí—that vast interior drainage in eastern Chihuahua and western Coahuila that had sheltered Indian resistance fighters since the 1600s—when Joaquín Terrazas and 260 Chihuahuans and Tarahumara Indians cornered him and shot him and seventy-seven of his people down on October 15, 1880. Sixty-eight of Victorio's band were taken prisoners.

Reign of Apaches

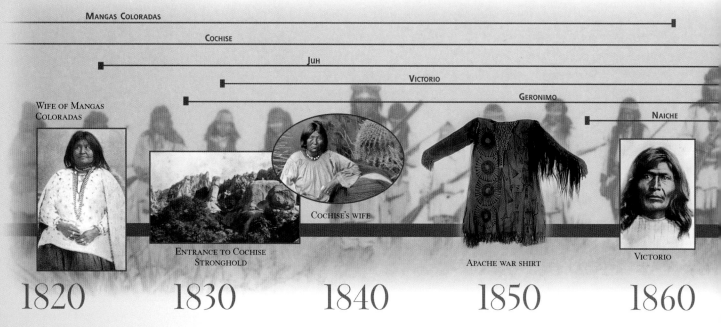

Mangas Coloradas

Cochise

Juh

Victorio

Geronimo

Naiche

Wife of Mangas Coloradas

Cochise's Wife

Entrance to Cochise Stronghold

Apache war shirt

Victorio

1820   1830   1840   1850   1860

The Apache wars are usually portrayed as a conflict between Indians and the U.S. cavalry. Yet many of the battles were fought on Mexican soil. Two years after Victorio's death, six-foot-tall, 225-pound Juh, chief of the Nednhi band of the Western Apaches, lured a group of soldiers stationed at Galeana in northwestern Chihuahua into an ambush. While holding off a Mexican relief column, Juh and his men killed Juan Mata Ortiz, Terraza's second-in-command, and all but one of his troops. The following year, Chihuahuans attacked Juh's camp and murdered his wife and daughter. Generations of Spaniards, Mexicans, and Apaches had grown up and died fighting one another. People on both sides could talk of a father killed here, a sister stolen there, a clansman scalped, a nephew mutilated. There were geopolitics involved—Chiricahuas like Mangas Coloradas and Cochise were master diplomats as well as warriors—but you also shed blood to avenge your kin.

The last of the great Chiricahua war leaders was Geronimo. Geronimo was never a chief, not even of his small Bedonkoke band. After Juh's death in 1883, the Chokonen and Nednhi Chiricahuas in the Sierra Madre followed Cochise's son Naiche. Geronimo was a shaman with great supernatural power, however. "No White Eyes seem to understand the importance of that in controlling Apaches," Juh's son Asa Daklugie recalled. "Naiche was not a Medicine Man; so he needed Geronimo as Geronimo needed him."

General Crook was the first to campaign against Naiche and Geronimo in Mexico after Mexico and the United States negotiated an agreement that U.S. forces could cross the border "in hot pursuit" of Indians. After Crook's force of fifty soldiers and 200 Quechan, Mohave, and Apache scouts pursued the Chiricahuas into

GERONIMO

GERONIMO SURRENDERING
TO GENERAL CROOK

NAICHE, COCHISE'S SON

GERONIMO IN OKLAHOMA

1870   1880   1890   1900   1910

APACHES BEING DEPORTED TO
FLORIDA. NAICHE IN CENTER
WITH GERONIMO TO THE RIGHT

OPPOSITE: CHIRICAHUA
MOUNTAINS, ARIZONA

their Sierra Madre strongholds, the Apaches agreed to return to the White Mountain Reservation. From February 1884 until May 1885, they farmed along Turkey Creek fifteen miles south of Fort Apache. But the prohibition of *tizwin*, a fermented corn liquor, and government interference with Apache family relationships under the guise of preventing wife-beating finally drove Geronimo, Naiche, and 132 other Chiricahuas back to Mexico.

Led by Chato and other Chiricahua scouts, Crook chased Geronimo in Sonora and Chihuahua again. The Chiricahuas refused the government's demand for unconditional surrender, however, so General Nelson Miles replaced Crook. Miles threw 5,000 soldiers—one-fourth of the entire U.S. army—into the fray, but two Chiricahua scouts—Kayitah and Martine under Lieutenant Charles Gatewood—tracked the Chiricahuas down. On September 4, 1886, Geronimo surrendered for the fourth and final time in Skeleton Canyon in the Peloncillo Mountains. He and his people were loaded into railroad cars and deported to prisons in Florida.

The U.S. government exiled Chato and the other scouts as well, a decision that infuriated Crook. **"The surrender of Geronimo could not have been effected except for the assistance of Chato and his scouts,"** Crook protested. "For their allegiance, they have been rewarded by captivity in a strange land." Crook spent the last years of his life fighting to resettle the Chiricahuas near Fort Sill in Oklahoma. He even visited them in Mount Vernon, Alabama, where they had been transferred after 119 of the 498 prisoners-of-war had died in malarial Florida jails. "Chatto [sic] came out, and went out to the General, and gave him a greeting that was really tender," one young officer reported. "It was a touching sight."

Crook died in 1890 while the Chiricahuas were still languishing in exile in the South. In 1894, the government allowed them to move to Fort Sill, where they organized themselves into "villages" that resembled their traditional local groups. Then, in 1913, the Chiricahuas were given a choice: private land in Oklahoma or part of the Mescalero reservation in New Mexico. After being gone from their Southwestern homelands for nearly thirty years, 187 of the 271 surviving Chiricahuas, including Chato, returned to mountains near the mountains of their youth.

Extraction

On January 1, 1879, former territorial delegate Miguel Otero drove a golden spike to celebrate the arrival of the Atchinson, Topeka, and Santa Fe Railroad in New Mexico. The Chiricahua Apaches were still at war, but the entrance of the railroad brought the Southwestern frontier face to face with the Industrial Age. Pushing south and west through Raton Pass, the Santa Fe reached New Mexico's capital in February 1880. The merchandise of the Santa Fe Trail now rode the iron rail.

Meanwhile, to the west, Charles Crocker drove his Chinese crews south from San Francisco down California's Central Valley. Then the Southern Pacific Railroad turned east and crossed the Colorado River, steaming into Tucson on March 20, 1880. That November, a Southern Pacific locomotive ran into two freight wagons belonging to Tully, Ochoa, and Company. That collision symbolized the end of the frontier. As the railroads let loose what one of their boosters called an "irresistible torrent of civilization and prosperity," the Southwest's mercantile economy sank beneath the flood. Both people and capital from the rest of the United States and Europe poured into the region. In New Mexico alone, property values rose from $41 million in 1880 to $231 million a decade later.

MINING COPPER

OPPOSITE: RANCHING AT YELLOWJACKET RANCH, UTAH

BACKGROUND: CHINESE RAILROAD WORKERS

THE RANCHERS

Among the first to feel this sea change were the ranchers. Stockraising had been a part of the Southwest since 1598, when Juan de Oñate's expedition colonized northern New Mexico. But even though sheepraising spread across northern New Mexico in the 1700s and early 1800s, ranching in Arizona remained hostage to Apache hostilities. Mission herds and Mexican land grants expanded in brief spurts only to contract violently. When Lieutenant Philip St. George Cooke and his Mormon Battalion crossed southeastern Arizona in 1846, the land grants had been abandoned and the cattle had all gone feral. By 1854, the wild cattle had disappeared. Most of the cattle and sheep supplying army posts in Arizona during the 1860s and early 1870s came from Sonora, New Mexico, or Texas.

Top: Mary Ann Goodnight, wife of rancher Charles Goodnight

Center: Cattle in snow

Opposite: Pecos valley, New Mexico

One of those early contractors was John Chisum, who followed the Goodnight-Loving Trail into New Mexico in 1867. A Tennessean who migrated to Texas, Chisum became the "Cattle King of the Pecos," establishing his headquarters on the South Spring River just below Roswell. During the 1870s, he ran as many as 80,000 head bearing his famous Jinglebob brand, selling cattle to reservations and military posts in New Mexico and Arizona. In 1875, he supplied 6,000 head to the San Carlos Reservation alone. He also fought bitterly with small ranchers and rustlers who were moving onto the unfenced public domain in southeastern New Mexico. Chisum was a product of the frontier–"a great trail man" in the words of legendary cattleman Charles Goodnight. He drove his herds onto the Pecos plains when they were still virgin grasslands.

LOADING CATTLE ONTO
RAILROAD CARS

He died in 1884, before those grasslands withered because of drought and
overgrazing. Chisum saw the railroads
arrive but he did not live long enough to
feel their consequences.

A rancher who did was Colin
Cameron, who bought the San Rafael de
la Zanja land grant on the Arizona-
Sonora border in 1882. Unlike Chisum,
Cameron never trailed a herd out of
Texas. On the contrary, he arrived in
Arizona on the Southern Pacific—a
Pennsylvanian with political connec-
tions in Washington, D.C., dressed in
Eastern clothes and carrying a walking
stick. Cameron represented a new breed of cattlegrower—an investor with Eastern
partners who viewed ranching as a business, not a way of life. Stockraisers like
Chisum came to the Southwest to supply army posts, Indian reservations, and
mining towns in the region itself. Businessmen like Cameron converted the grasses
of Arizona and New Mexico into beef on the hoof that could be loaded into railroad cars
and transported to California or the Midwest. The Southwest was the arena of production, not consumption.

Ironically, however, the major function of the railroads during the early 1880s
was to ship cattle into Arizona and New Mexico, not to export them. Promotional litera-
ture like Patrick Hamilton's *Resources of Arizona*, published in San Francisco in 1883,
touted Arizona as a stockraiser's paradise where "even in the driest season the feed
never fails, and the owner can sit in the shade of his comfortable hacienda and see his
herds thrive and increase winter and summer." Investors from the United States and
Europe stocked the Southwest with hundreds of thousands of cattle and sheep. In 1870,
the territorial governor reported that Arizona had only 5,132 cattle, even though pioneer ranchers estimated there were perhaps 38,000 head on the range. By 1883, there
were 652,500, and by the early 1890s, there were perhaps 1,500,000 cattle and more than
a million sheep. During the 1880s, New Mexico's cattle herds skyrocketed from 347,000
to 1,630,000. Grass was gold. The range was open and endless. Or so it seemed.

The Pecos country crashed first. In the winter of 1885–86, not much snow fell. The following spring was dry. Grass withered and cattle had to range farther and farther for feed. Thousands starved. Others, crazed with thirst, staggered back to the Pecos and plunged over its steep banks. Carcasses rotted in the water and screw worms proliferated. Drinking water had to be strained through gunny sacks because there were so many maggots. Frank Lloyd, a Jinglebob cowboy, claimed that nearly half the cattle in the country died that year. Many small outfits went belly up, while larger ones like George Littlefield's LFD, which dominated the range north of the Jinglebob, moved east onto the Llano Estacado in Texas. The Pecos was earning its reputation as the Graveyard of the Cowman's Hopes.

Arizona ranchers also suffered during the 1885 drought, but the cattle boom in Arizona did not go bust until the drought of 1891–93. The three-year dry spell hit at a time when Arizona ranges were disastrously overstocked. "There are valleys over which one can ride for several miles without finding mature grasses sufficient for herbarium specimens without searching under bushes or in similar places," botanist J. W. Toumey of the Arizona Experiment Station observed. Yet even though most cattle ranchers saw the danger, few reduced their herds. According to Colin Cameron, "Men with many thousands of dollars at stake, knowing that we have only 40,000,000 acres of grazing land (and that a very large portion of this, by reason of great distance from drinking water, was not available), that it requires 15 to 25 acres of feed to one animal, made no effort to sell or remove even a part of their stock, but continued on in the even tenor of their way, expecting that the coming year would furnish grass to meet the necessity of the occasion."

But 1892 was almost as dry as 1891. Cattle, sheep, and horses began dying in May and June. Ranchers did not start shipping their animals out of the territory until later that summer or fall. "I was busy dragging half-dead cattle out of the spring mudholes, shooting motherless calves and looking for rain, which did not come," recalled Fred Alkire, who ranched along New River north of Phoenix. The die-off was even worse in southern Arizona, where 50 to 75 percent of the cattle perished. Soon a new industry arose, "which the cowboys looked upon with much disgust—almost akin to grave robbing," wrote J. P. Gray, who ran cattle in the Chiricahua Mountains. "That was the business of the sun-bleached bones of the drought victims. Near almost every railroad station there were accumulated great stacks of bones hauled in from cattle ranges." The bones were gathered to be ground into fertilizer. They were stark reminders of a Southwestern tragedy of the commons on the open range: the price both ranchers and the land paid for unregulated grazing on the public domain.

From Forest Reserves to the Taylor Grazing Act

The federal government first attempted to regulate the Southwestern commons in the early1890s, when it established the Pecos and Grand Canyon Forest Reserves. A decade later, President Teddy Roosevelt expanded the reserves into the national forests that dominate the highland Southwest today. By 1908, 13,385,990 acres in Arizona and 8,474,547 acres of New Mexico fell within their boundaries.

During most of the nineteenth century, the U.S. government had devised a number of ways to make the public domain private. By the early twentieth century, the greatest experiment in public land management had begun. From the very beginning, controversy raged over who would have access to these vast tracts of timber and grasslands. "Cattle-Free in '93" was a slogan during the debate over public lands ranching in the early 1990s. A hundred years earlier, the first regulation concerning the forest reserves prohibited the "driving, feeding, grazing, pasturing, or herding of cattle, sheep, or other livestock" on those lands. For the next eight years, preservationists like John Muir pressured their allies in the Department of the Interior to run the ranchers off the reserves. A report by Gifford Pinchot and Fredrick Colville of the Department of Agriculture, which argued that properly managed grazing did not damage the forests, was suppressed.

CONSERVATIONIST
TEDDY ROOSEVELT AND
PRESERVATIONIST JOHN MUIR

BACKGROUND: CATTLE IN
ARROYO

OPPOSITE: SANDIA MOUN-
TAINS BY THE RIO GRANDE,
NEW MEXICO

But Pinchot, who believed that natural resources should be conserved in order to rationalize their use, was a friend of Teddy Roosevelt, who became president after McKinley was assassinated in 1901. Roosevelt rescinded the order expelling cattle and sheep from the reserves. In 1905, he even transferred the reserves to the Department of Agriculture's new Bureau of Forestry, headed by Pinchot. The preservation of wilderness took a back seat to the concept of multiple use. The Forest Service developed a system of grazing allotments and per-head fees to regulate, not eliminate, grazing on national forests.

That system was not extended to the rest of the federal public domain for another three decades. In 1934, reeling from drought and the devastation of the Dust Bowl, Congress passed the Taylor Grazing Act. The purpose of the legislation was to **"stop injury to the public grazing lands by preventing overgrazing and soil deterioration, to provide for their orderly use, improvement, and development, to stabilize the livestock industry dependent upon the public range, and for other uses."** Fifty years after the explosion of the cattle industry in the 1880s, the era of the open range had finally come to an end in the Southwest.

THE MINERS

Photographs of Arizona and New Mexico at the end of the nineteenth century reveal an almost lunar landscape in places. Part of the problem was the devastating intersection of drought and overgrazing. But another extractive industry—mining—contributed as much or more to the denuding of Southwestern hillsides and floodplains. Until the 1890s, the mining industry relied almost exclusively upon cordwood to fuel the steam engines that powered pumps, hoists, stamps, ore crushers, smelters, and every other stage in the mining process. Woodcutters fanned out across the countryside, cutting

ENORMOUS QUANTITIES OF WOOD TO FUEL THE SILVER KING MINE IN ARIZONA

OPPOSITE: ED SCHIEFFELIN

down mesquite bosques along watercourses and stripping the evergreen woodlands of oak, pinyon, and juniper. Geographers Conrad Bahre and Charles Hutchinson calculated that the Tombstone mines alone consumed 120,000 to 130,000 cords of wood between 1879 and 1886. Stacked four feet high in eight-foot lengths, those cords would have stretched for 200 miles.

Mining by its very nature was a boom-and-bust industry. During the early territorial period, placer gold strikes at Gila City (1857) in southwestern Arizona and Pinos Altos in southwestern New Mexico (1860) lured several thousand prospectors to the Southwestern frontier. "The earth was turned inside out," journalist J. Ross Browne wrote of Gila City. "Rumors of extraordinary discoveries flew on the wings of the wind in every direction. Enterprising men hurried to the spot with barrels of whiskey and billiard tables; Jews came with ready-made clothing and fancy wares; traders crowded in with wagon-loads of pork and beans; and gamblers came with cards and monte-tables. **There was everything in Gila City within a few months but a church and a jail, which were accounted barbarisms by the mass of the population.**"

These placer boom towns faded as quickly as they flared. When Browne revisited Gila City in 1864, "the promising Metropolis of Arizona consisted of three chimneys and a coyote." But after the alluvial deposits had been panned or dry-winnowed, miners began to probe subsurface lodes and veins. Solitary prospectors often discovered the gold- or silver-bearing ore, but investors with capital to sink the shafts and build the mills usually developed the mines. Thousands of men and even a few women braved the Arizona and New Mexico deserts searching for their own bonanzas. Most ended up working for wages in company mines and mills.

A classic case in point was Tombstone, Arizona. In 1877, a habitual prospector named Ed Schieffelin drifted into the San Pedro Valley. Soldiers at Camp Huachuca fighting the Chiricahua Apaches told Schieffelin the only thing he would find was his tombstone. "The word lingered in my mind," Schieffelin later reminisced, "and when I got into the country where Tombstone is now located, I gave the name to the first location that I made."

That discovery became the biggest silver strike in South-western history. During the Tombstone boom, which lasted until 1886, at least fifty mines produced $20 to $30 million in silver, equal to about $230 to $350 million today. By 1880, Tombstone itself was a community of 10,000–12,000 people. Hundreds of miners blasted ore out of the tunnels, which teamsters transported to stamp mills along the San Pedro River in huge wagons pulled by sixteen to twenty mules. Hundreds of millworkers then shoveled the ore into waterpowered rockbreakers that pulverized it into powder that could be mixed with mercury in pans. Finally, furnacemen reduced the amal-gam until the mercury vaporized and left a residue of silver behind.

It was a hard and dangerous way to make a living. Hardrock miners plunged down shafts in cages that fell 800 feet a minute. Exposed to mercury poisoning, furnacemen had to loop ropes around their legs and necks to keep themselves from twitching when they went to sleep. After working as an ore shoveler and turning down a furnaceman's job, young Sam Aaron wrote, "The first opportunity I had I started to be a faro-dealer." Schieffelin himself sold his claims and left Tombstone in 1880, wandering from Alaska to Oregon in search of "somewhere that has wealth, for the digging of it. I like the excitement of being right up against the earth, trying to coax her gold away and scatter it."

EARLY
MINER'S HELMET

OPPOSITE: THE FORMER MINING
TOWN OF JEROME, ARIZONA

HARD ROCK MINERS IN TOMB-
STONE

When most people think of Tombstone, they think of Wyatt Earp and the Gun-fight at the O.K. Corral. But the important developments took place below ground, where the ore that financed the boom was mined. Perhaps Tombstone's most neglected story is the role it played in Western labor history. Responding to falling silver prices, mine owners slashed wages from four dollars a day to three in 1884. For two decades, the four-dollar day had been the pride of Western hardrock miners, so in May, 300 of Tombstone's 400 miners organized the Tomb-stone Miners' Union and went on strike. At first, most residents supported the strikers. But after the companies closed down Tombstone's three largest mines and everyone's income suffered, public opinion turned against the miners. Deputy sheriffs from Cochise County and federal troops from Fort Huachuca marched into Tombstone to keep order and protect the mines. By the end of the hot Arizona summer, the strike had withered. By 1885, the four-dollar day was collapsing across the West.

The Good, the Bad, and the Mythological:
Wyatt Earp and the Wild West

WYATT EARP

VIRGIL EARP

MORGAN EARP

Like Billy the Kid, Wyatt Earp has far more mythological than historical importance. During the 1870s, after his first wife died of typhoid, Earp worked as a police officer in the Kansas cattle towns of Wichita and Dodge City, where he became close friends with Doc Holliday and Bat Masterson. Cowboys called Earp and Masterson the "Fighting Pimps" because they spent much of their time in whorehouses and saloons.

Earp followed his brothers to Tombstone in 1880 at the height of the boom, gambling and working as a bouncer in the Oriental Saloon. His brother Virgil served as town marshal. Tombstone's reputation for lawlessness was well-deserved; according to lawyer Wells Spicer, there were **"two dance houses, a dozen gambling places, over twenty saloons, and more than five hundred gamblers"** in town. The Earps quickly became part of a faction that included former San Carlos

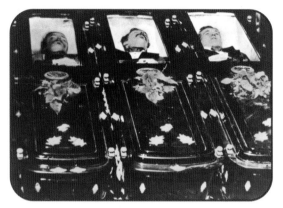

TOM AND FRANK MCLOWERY AND BILLY CLANTON

Apache agent John Clum, editor of the *Tombstone Epitaph*. Their enemies were the shady Tombstone Townsite Company and the "Texas Cowboys," including Curly Bill Brocius and the Clanton family.

What happened next was not the Western morality play of pulp fiction or Hollywood stereotype. On October 26, 1881, the Clantons squared off against Wyatt, Morgan, and Virgil Earp and Doc Holliday at the O.K. Corral. Three members of the Clanton gang died in the gunfight. The townspeople suspended Virgil Earp as marshal; two months later, he was ambushed and crippled. In March 1882, the Texas Cowboys murdered Morgan Earp. Wyatt, his brother Warren, and Doc Holliday hunted down and killed at least two of the suspects. Then they fled to Colorado, where tuberculosis finally killed Doc Holliday in 1887. Wyatt spent the rest of his long life drifting from police work to gambling to prospecting. He died in Los Angeles in 1929.

Earp's friend John Clum considered him "quite my ideal of the strong, manly, serious and capable peace officer." His sister-in-law Allie believed he was a compulsive gambler who forced the gunfight at the O.K. Corral because he and the Clantons had robbed a stage together. Depending on which of Wyatt's contemporaries you believe, he was either a hero or a murderous bully.

The truth was probably gray, not black or white. Earp, like other violent men, moved from one frontier town to another looking for an easy way to make a living. Some, like Billy the Kid, ran afoul of the law. Others, like Earp, straddled it. Both were reflections of their region and time.

"BABY PONY," WYATT EARP'S REVOLVER
BACKGROUND: TOMBSTONE FROM
COMSTOCK HILL, 1879

KING COPPER

*S*ilver and gold may have fueled the early development of mining in the Southwest, but copper, not precious metals, turned the region into an extractive colony of industrial America. By the 1880s, the Electrical Age had arrived, generating an enormous demand for copper conducting wire. As the cities of the eastern United States swathed themselves in electrical lines, engineers backed by eastern and European capital probed every corner of the West, searching for the ore that lighted and powered industries and homes.

They found much of that copper in the Southwest, where the important districts of Hurley–Santa Rita in New Mexico and Clifton-Morenci, Bisbee-Douglas, Globe-Miami, Ray, Jerome, and Ajo in Arizona developed. After a few early strikes, Southwestern copper mining depended upon corporate capitalism, not individual

prospectors. "Copper was mined by the ton, like iron or coal," historian Philip Mellinger notes. "The quest for shiny blue-green rock with 20 or even 30 percent copper soon shifted to a search for lower grade ore, in which less than 5 percent metal content was sufficient for profitability." That quest required millions of dollars of investment in mines, mills, smelters, and transportation networks, particularly railroads. It also demanded a large and stable workforce trained to do many different tasks.

MEXICAN COPPER MINERS
IN ARIZONA

The workforce itself resembled the immigrant Babel reshaping industrial regions in the eastern United States. There were Anglo Americans, Cornishmen ("Cousin Jacks"), Germans, Irishmen, Italians, Spaniards, and Slavs from Serbia and Croatia. And there were Mexicans from Arizona, Sonora, and Chihuahua. Company managers in Clifton-Morenci even tried to import Chinese laborers in the early 1880s. "If occasionally a few were killed no questions were asked, and the work went on as usual," mine manager James Colquhoun callously observed. But Anglo and Mexican workers joined to drive the Chinese out of the mines and off the railroads, beating or killing them, stealing their money, and burning their homes.

Many Anglo Irish miners (from the United States and the British Isles) then attempted to keep the best paying jobs for themselves. Anglo Irish and Mexican workers occasionally united to pursue higher wages, shorter hours, and safer workplaces. But differences of ethnicity and race undercut uniformities of class in the mining towns of the Southwest. Those differences were one of the reasons why the copper companies were able to turn back organized labor's charge and gut the unions during World War I.

The mining companies deliberately aggravated those ethnic differences by mixing their workforces. "The Unions cannot hold peoples from different countries together into a solid mass," one coal-company executive said. The corporations also paid Mexican, Spanish, Italian, and Slavic workers lower wages for the same jobs than Anglo American, Irish, British, or Northern European miners. Most divisive of all their tactics, however, was the use of different ethnic groups as strike breakers. And since mining districts in Arizona and New Mexico were so close to the Mexican border, the ready supply of Mexican labor reinforced the stereotype that Mexicans were scabs. The Western Federation of Miners, the strongest union in the West during the early twentieth century, often excluded Mexicans from its organizing campaigns.

THE CLIFTON-MORENCI STRIKE

El Paso: Northern Gateway

*M*any of those Mexican immigrants came to the Southwest through the old colonial town of El Paso, Texas, on the Rio Grande. Between 1880 and 1920, El Paso transformed itself from a border hamlet to the largest port of entry along the U.S.–Mexican border. In the words of historian Mario García, **"El Paso symbolized to Mexicans what New York had represented to European immigrants: the opening to what they believed would be a better life."**

There were both pull and push factors involved. The expansion of the Southwest's extractive economy demanded labor in ranching, agriculture, and mining. The construction of the El Paso Smelter in 1887 drew gold, silver, lead, and copper ore from both Mexico and the United States, most of it shipped on the five major railroads that converged on the community in the early 1880s. By World War I, the smelter employed as many as 3,000 workers, many of them Mexican immigrants. Jobs in El Paso and the rest of the Southwest turned many eyes northward.

ABOVE: MEXICAN RAIL WORKERS

CENTER: EL PASO TODAY

BACKGROUND: MEXICAN LABORERS IN FIELD WITH SCYTHES

Despite racism and institutionalized discrimination, life in the United States was often seen as the only option to grinding poverty or death for many Mexicans during those difficult years. Under Porfirio Díaz, who ruled Mexico from 1876 until he was overthrown in 1910, thousands of Indians and campesinos (country people) lost their communal lands to large landowners or foreign corporations. Debt peonage flourished on the haciendas that dominated the Mexican countryside. To escape, Mexicans from northern and central Mexico crossed the deserts and the Rio Grande to *el otro lado* ("the other side"). Many others fled the carnage that followed during the Mexican Revolution (1910–1920), when 1.5 to 2 million of Mexico's population of approximately 15 million—one in every eight Mexicans—died because of revolutionary violence and civil war. The refugees rode the Mexican Central Railroad north from Mexico City, Zacatecas, Chihuahua City, and hundreds of smaller stops along the way, working in the El Paso smelter, the cotton fields of Arizona, the orchards of the Pacific Northwest, the ranches of New Mexico, and even the automobile factories of Detroit. The modern Southwest could not have been built without their labor and skill.

Town of Morenci

Below: Arrested strikers
Abrán Salcido, Juan de la O,
and Francisco Salerni

Opposite: Bisbee's Lavender
Mine

Nonetheless, Mexican, Italian, and Spanish workers mounted the first major strike in the Southwest. The strike broke out in Clifton-Morenci in June 1903 after the Arizona territorial legislature passed the eight-hour day with no cut in daily pay. When the law was passed, Clifton-Morenci was the only major Arizona mining district where miners still worked ten-hour shifts. Its labor force was also largely Mexican and Southern European rather than Anglo Irish. The law was therefore an indirect attack on "alien," that is, Mexican, labor as well as a protective measure for labor itself. In the words of historian Joseph Park, the eight-hour law was designed to be "an effective blow delivered to mine operators who sought to employ alien Mexicans whenever possible because they would submit to working ten to twelve hours a day at a wage that undercut the union scale by about 50 percent."

Phelps Dodge challenged the Western Federation of Miners and its supporters in the territorial legislature by reducing the work day to eight hours but only paying for nine rather than ten hours. This circumvention of the law effectively slashed daily wages by 10 percent. Soon the Clifton-Morenci's Mexican and Southern European workforce began picketing the mines, where they demanded equal pay for equal work as well. One Anglo resident observed that it was **"a pretty big crowd—mostly Mexicans, but a lot of Dagoes, Bohunks, and foreigners of different kinds ... no whites at all."**

Since the Western Federation of Miners had ignored the district because of its ethnic composition, the strikers coordinated their activities through their *mutualistas*, or mutual-aid societies. Strike leaders included Mexicans Abrán Salcido, Juan de la O, and Severo Montez along with Italian Francisco Salerni and Weneslado Laustaunau, who, despite his surname, was a Mexican immigrant. To suppress the strike, the copper companies convinced the territorial governor to call in fifty Graham County sheriff deputies, the entire contingent of the Arizona Rangers, 230 Arizona National Guardsmen, and a unit of the U.S. Cavalry—the largest military force assembled in Arizona since the Apache wars.

Enrolling Hispanics into the Union

Early summer rains aided this occupying army by sending floodwaters surging through Clifton. Perhaps fifty people drowned. In the sodden, sullen aftermath of the strike, ten Mexican and Italian strike leaders were convicted of rioting and locked up in Yuma Territorial Prison.

After Clifton-Morenci, the Western Federation of Miners attempted to bring Mexican and Southern European workers into the union in Bisbee, Jerome, and Globe. But many Anglo Irish miners continued to view "the foreigners" with suspicion and contempt. As Arizona approached statehood, a coalition between organized labor and progressive small business people dominated the constitutional convention and wrote many pro-labor provisions into the constitution. Union delegates also tried to exclude "alien labor" from public work projects, mandate that at least 80 percent of an enterprise's workforce had to be English-speaking citizens, and prohibit anyone who could not "speak the English language" from working in "underground or other hazardous occupations," that is, in the mines or on the railroads, the best paying jobs in the territory. These measures were defeated, but after Arizona became a state in 1912, organized labor sponsored the 80 percent clause as an initiative. Arizonans approved it by more than 10,000 votes. The U.S. Supreme Court struck the clause down in 1915.

Forging the Copper Collar

In 1915, as copper prices skyrocketed during World War I, Anglo Irish, Mexican, and Southern European workers set aside their differences and won a series of strikes in Miami, Ray, and Clifton-Morenci. But the copper companies, led by Walter Douglas of Phelps Dodge, also worked together to mount a counteroffensive. It culminated in 1917, when patriotic fervor and wartime fears of foreigners and sabotage turned many Americans against the unions. On July 11, Douglas, vice-president of Phelps Dodge, spoke at an anti-strike rally in Globe. **"There will be no compromise because you cannot compromise with a rattlesnake,"** Douglas thundered. **"I believe the government will be able to show that there is German influence behind this movement. It is up to the individual communities to drive these agitators out as has been done in other communities in the past."**

A day later, in Douglas's own community of Bisbee, 2,000 vigilantes deputized by Sheriff Henry Wheeler of Cochise County broke into homes and boardinghouses and arrested strikers at 6:30 a.m. Without benefit of court hearing or legal counsel, the vigilantes then marched 2,000 strikers to the Warren Ball Park, and gave them the choice to renounce the strike or be deported. Eight hundred miners agreed to go back to work, but 1,186 refused. These men were loaded into twenty-three boxcars from the El Paso & Southwestern Railroad and shipped out of town. Fifteen hours later, the cramped and thirsty deportees jumped down from the boxcars. It was 3:00 a.m. They had no food or water. The vigilantes had abandoned them in the middle of the desert at Hermanas, New Mexico.

BISBEE DEPORTATION, 1917

BACKGROUND: DEPORTEES ARE MARCHED THROUGH BISBEE TO RAIL CARS BY VIGILANTES

The Bisbee Deportation appalled President Woodrow Wilson, who ordered the army to set up a camp for the men at Columbus, New Mexico. Then he appointed a federal commission to investigate the action. In 1918, the U.S. Department of Justice even charged twenty-one Cochise County officials and Phelps Dodge executives, including Sheriff Wheeler and Walter Douglas, with conspiracy and kidnapping. After Phelps Dodge attorneys successfully argued that the case should be moved from federal to state courts, however, all defendants were acquitted. During the conservative 1920s, independent unionism withered in the Southwestern copper towns as the copper companies forged the "copper collar" and controlled Arizona politics. During the Depression of the 1930s, many mines closed. Miners did not throw off the copper collar until 1946, when returning Mexican American veterans of World War II revived the unions and forced Phelps Dodge and other companies to end the dual wage system.

Lungers and Tourists

*D*uring the early twentieth century, new enterprises such as cotton farming in Arizona and oil drilling in New Mexico joined established extractive industries like ranching and copper mining to dominate the Southwestern economy. Many homesteaders also struggled to dry farm New Mexico's eastern plains. In Roosevelt County alone, the population rose from 3,000 people in 1904 to more than 12,000 in 1910. Three-fourths of those homesteaders lost their land as the dry farming boom went bust during the drought years of 1909 to 1912.

For the first time since the region became a part of the United States, however, the Southwest attracted other newcomers for reasons that had nothing to do with what they could rip or raise from the ground. Some came for the climate, others for the natural beauty or cultural heritage. Together they gave the Southwest a new identity–one based on the region's intrinsic qualities rather than commodity production.

Among the first to arrive were the health-seekers. At a time when tuberculosis caused 12 of every 100 deaths in the United States and was the leading cause of death in the industrializing world of North America and Europe, a desperate pilgrimage of "lungers, consumptives, phthisics, coughers, hackers, invalids, valetudinarians, sanitarians, asthmatics, rheumatics, white plaguers, pukers, and walking death," in the words of historian Billy M. Jones, streamed west to cure their respiratory ailments in the dry, desert air. Some, like future Senator Clinton P. Anderson of New Mexico, survived and prospered. Others coughed away their lives in miserable tent cities on the outskirts of cities like Albuquerque, Phoenix, and Tucson. Many of the first resorts and hospitals in the Southwest opened to cater to or care for the lungers.

Opposite: Sonoran Desert in bloom

Letterhead from Montezuma Hot Springs resort

The railroads, chiefly the Atchison, Topeka, and Santa Fe, introduced another group—tourists—to the region. Despite being given millions of acres of land in Arizona and New Mexico, the Santa Fe never figured out how to make the Southwest pay during the 1880s and 1890s. In 1893, however, Fred Harvey signed an exclusive contract with the railroad to provide dining car service west of Kansas City. Three years later, Edward Ripley took over a reorganized Santa Fe and began to promote the Southwest as a destination rather than a long, desolate stretch on the way to California. The Grand Canyon was the biggest draw after the Santa Fe built a spur line from Williams to the South Rim in 1901. But the austere grandeur of Navajo Country and the pinyon-scented highlands of northern New Mexico enticed tourists as well. To serve those customers, Fred Harvey Company and the Santa Fe Railway built a series of hotels, such as El Tovar at the Grand Canyon and La Posada in Winslow, Arizona, that not only provided comfort but defined Southwestern style for thousands of travelers along the line. Many of those structures and their interiors were designed by Mary Elizabeth Jane Colter, a pioneering woman architect in a male field. According to Matilda McQuaid and Karen Bartlett, **"Colter's passion for authenticity helped to re-create Native American and pioneer life and to frame the dramatic landscapes of the Grand Canyon and the Painted Desert from her buildings."**

The federal government played a major role in this repackaging of the Southwest. Between 1892 and 1907, U.S. presidents set aside twenty-five forest reserves and four national forests under the General Land Law Revision Act of 1891.

Top: Tourists buying wares from Indians

Above: Fred Harvey

Opposite: Aerial view of the Grand Canyon, Grand Canyon National Park, Arizona

DESERT VIEW, GRAND CANYON,
DESIGNED BY MARY COLTER

EARLY POSTCARD

An ardent conservationist, Teddy Roosevelt was notably active, proclaiming a series of national monuments like Petrified Forest (1906), Montezuma Castle (1906), El Morro (1906), Chaco Canyon (1907), and Tumacacori (1908) as well. The Southwest's cultural as well as natural treasures were being withdrawn from the public domain and protected from pothunting and vandalism. These archaeological and historical sites intrigued and entranced tourists almost as much as the immense vistas of the Grand Canyon or the majestic peaks of the Sangre de Cristos.

By the 1920s, another mode of transportation—the automobile—was revolutionizing tourism in the Southwest. The number of tourists at the Grand Canyon rose from 56,335 in 1920 to 162,715 a decade later. Many of those tourists rode the Santa Fe, but by 1927, railroad tourists represented less than half the visitors to the South Rim. The Southwest's dependence upon the automobile had begun.

Some of the tourists just came to stare. Others, in contrast, wanted to play cowboy and Indian. Dude ranches sprang up

across Arizona and New Mexico, many with amenities such as tennis courts and polo fields as well as horses and wranglers. And while some were working cattle outfits, the fancier establishments drew Easterners west to "meet nature in her ruggedness and still lead a 'white-man's life.'"

Many of those leading a 'white-man's life' also grew fascinated with Indian ways. Mary Colter designed Hopi House for the Fred Harvey Company at the Grand Canyon. There Hopi and Navajo artists sold their jewelry, pots, and blankets, performing dances for the tourists as well. Even more ambitious travelers hopped aboard "Harveycoaches" or "Harveycars" and embarked upon "Indian Detours" to New Mexico Pueblos or Navajo settlements. One of the most popular Detours brought tourists to the Hopi Snake Dance, which became the most publicized Indian ritual in the Southwest. The line between tourism and intrusion was often a fine one. **"Those who sang and danced for the tourists at hotels far away from home eventually found those seekers appearing in the plazas, demanding to see the authentic dances on feast days,"** Rayna Green, Director of the American Indian Program at the National Museum of American History, wryly commented. "The social dances offered them—the horsetail, Comanche, Eagle, Friendship, skip, and two-step dances—were no longer sufficient for the intrepid ones, who pushed their way into the pueblos and hogans, climbed the kiva ladders, and insisted on watching the pots fired and the bread baked."

The Scientists

*A*mong those "intrepid ones" were anthropologists and archaeologists who saw the Southwest as an enormous natural laboratory to study human diversity from antiquity to the present. Some, like Frank Hamilton Cushing, did indeed push their way into kivas with little regard for the sensibilities of the people they wanted to observe. But others, including Cushing himself later in his career, made sincere and systematic efforts to record the lifeways and beliefs of the Hopis, Zunis, Rio Grande Pueblos, Navajos, Apaches, O'odham, and other Native peoples of the region. Many of these early scholars were women like Matilda Cox Stevenson, Florence Hawley Ellis, Gladys Reichard, and Ruth Underhill.

Meanwhile, archaeologists like Adolph Bandelier, Jesse Walter Fewkes, Earl Morris, Alfred Kidder, and Neil Judd were probing Southwestern ruins, trying to link the brooding past of Pueblo Grande, Aztec Ruins, Pecos, or Pueblo Bonito to the living present of the O'odham or the Pueblo people. Major breakthroughs in archaeological method and theory, such as stratigraphic digging, ceramic crossdating, and dendrochronology, or tree-ring dating, took place on Southwestern digs or in Southwestern laboratories.

ABOVE: ANCIENT POTTERY OF KEET SEEL, NAVAJO NATIONAL MONUMENT, ARIZONA

CENTER: *Left to right:* FLORENCE HAWLEY ELLIS, GLADYS PHACE, EMIL HAURY, AND CLARA LEE TANNER AT BANDELIER NATIONAL MONUMENT IN NEW MEXICO

BACKGROUND: BANDELIER NATIONAL MONUMENT, NEW MEXICO

OPPOSITE: CHACO CULTURE NATIONAL HISTORICAL PARK, NEW MEXICO

WATER CONTROL AND THE
TRANSFORMATION OF THE SOUTHWEST

*H*istorian Gerald Nash contends that it would have taken forty years of peace to transform the West as profoundly as four years of war did. Certainly, Arizona and New Mexico on the eve of World War II bore little resemblance to the region twenty years later. Both states remained more rural than urban; the three largest cities were Phoenix, with a population of 65,414, Tucson, with 36,818, and Albuquerque, with 35,449. Moreover, Arizona and New Mexico were still wedded to extractive industries at a time when farming, ranching, and mining suffered terribly during the Depression of the 1930s. Drought and declining cattle prices forced many cattle ranchers out of business, especially the smaller outfits. The Dust Bowl billowed into eastern New Mexico, causing the value of farm land to plummet to $4.95 an acre, the lowest in the nation. Cotton production in Arizona continued to grow, but in the winter of 1937–38, more than 37,000 migrant workers, most of them Okie and Arkie refugees from the Dust Bowl, found themselves stranded in the Salt River Valley when heavy rains in California destroyed crops. Meanwhile, the copper industry collapsed twice during the decade, throwing thousands of miners and smelter workers from Jerome to El Paso out of work. Entire districts like Ajo and Ray, Arizona, closed down, turning copper towns into ghost towns, at least for a time.

THRESHING MACHINE AT THE
GHOST TOWN OF PINOS
ALTOS, NEW MEXICO

OPPOSITE: SALT RIVER
CANYON WILDERNESS,
ARIZONA

Nonetheless, the transformation engendered by World War II and the postwar boom did not happen in a vacuum. New Deal programs like the Works Progress Administration (WPA) and the Civilian Conservation Corps (CCC) employed thousands of men and women who built roads, trails, parks, and public buildings, including many at the University of New Mexico, the University of Arizona, and Arizona State University. Much of the infrastructure that allowed the boom to take place was constructed by these federal programs.

But the foundation of the Southwest's explosive growth was laid even earlier, particularly in the Salt River Valley, the greatest conjunction of arable land and surface river water in the region. Along the Salt and Gila rivers, the pre-Hispanic Hohokam Indians developed the most extensive irrigation system in the Americas north of coastal Peru. Thousands of farmers and speculators followed the traces of Hohokam canals and turned the Salt River Valley into the "Garden of the Territory." During the 1890s, however, severe droughts alternated with devastating floods along the Salt River. Acreage in cultivation declined from 127,512 acres in 1896 to 96,863 acres a decade later. Farmers and canal companies went bankrupt. Banks failed. Future politicians like Carl Hayden, who served Arizona in the U.S. Congress from 1912 until 1969, stood guard over the family's irrigation headgates with his mother, who cradled a shotgun. To Southwesterners like Hayden, wild rivers were dangerous and capricious enemies. They dreamed of webs of dams and canals to reclaim the desert and make it bloom.

Their chance soon came when Congress passed the National Reclamation Act in 1902 and set up the Reclamation Service. One of its first major projects was to tame the Salt River by building an enormous dam northeast of Phoenix. Construction began in 1905. When it was completed in 1911, former president Teddy Roosevelt called Roosevelt Dam one of the "two greatest achievements of his administration." The other was the Panama Canal. The dam not only controlled flooding but impounded water in Roosevelt Lake, releasing it during dry periods. Salt River Valley farmers no longer reeled

ROOSEVELT DAM

OPPOSITE: ROOSEVELT LAKE, ARIZONA

from flood to drought. The cotton boom of World War I, where acreage in long-staple cotton necessary for automobile tires soared from 7,300 acres in 1916 to 180,000 in 1920, would not have been possible without the Reclamation Service's Salt River Project and Roosevelt Dam.

After World War II, Salt River Project canals brought water to Phoenix homes and businesses. The same dams that diverted water into those canals also produced hydroelectric power. The Salt River Project may have started as an agrarian dream to make fields of cotton, citrus, and vegetables rise from the ashes of the Hohokam. During the postwar boom, however, it transformed metropolitan Phoenix into the largest urban center between Los Angeles and Dallas–Fort Worth. Urban dreams replaced rural visions. Arizona and New Mexico moved from the Southwest to the Sunbelt as the frontier faded into myth and the era of extraction faded into the countryside, dwarfed by city life and city industries.

PHOENIX TODAY

OPPOSITE: CHACO CANYON

SUGGESTED READINGS

Bahre, Conrad. *A Legacy of Change: Historic Human Impact on Vegetation of the Arizona Borderlands.* Tucson: University of Arizona Press, 1991.

Beck, Warren. *New Mexico: A History of Four Centuries.* Norman: University of Oklahoma, 1971.

Browne, J. Ross. *Adventures in Apache Country: A Tour through Arizona and Sonora.* Tuscon: University of Arizona Press, 1982.

Byrkit, James W. *Forging the Copper Collar: Arizona's Labor-Management War 1901–1921.* Tucson: University of Arizona Press, 1982.

Eisenhower, John S.D. *So Far From God: The U.S. War With Mexico 1846–1848.* New York: Doubleday, 1989.

García, Mario. *Desert Immigrants: The Mexicans of El Paso, 1880–1920.* New Haven: Yale University Press, 1981.

Green, Rayna. "We Never Saw These Things Before: Southwest Indian Laughter and Resistance to the Invasion of the Tse va ho." In *The Great Southwest of the Fred Harvey Company and the Santa Fe Railway,* edited by Marta Weigle and Barbara A. Babcock. Phoenix: The Heard Museum, 1996.

Griswold del Castillo, Richard. *The Treaty of Guadalupe Hidalgo: A Legacy of Conflict.* Norman: University of Oklahoma Press, 1990.

Jones, Billy. *Health-Seekers in the Southwest, 1817–1900.* Norman: University of Oklahoma Press, 1967.

Marks, Paula. *And Die in the West: The Story of the O.K. Corral Gunfight.* New York: William Morrow and Company, Inc., 1989.

McQuaid, Matilda with Karen Bartlett. "Building an Image of the Southwest: Mary Colter, Fred Harvey Company, Architect." In *The Great Southwest of the Fred Harvey Company and the Santa Fe Railway,* edited by Marta Weigle and Barbara A. Babcock. Phoenix: The Heard Museum, 1996.

Mellinger, Philip J. *Race and Labor in Western Copper: The Fight for Equality, 1896–1918.* Tucson: University of Arizona Press, 1995.

Miller, Darlis. *Soldiers and Settlers: Military Supply in the Southwest, 1861–1885.* Albuquerque: University of New Mexico Press, 1989.

Nash, Gerald. *The American West Transformed: The Impact of the Second World War.* Bloomington: Indiana University Press, 1985.

Officer, James E. *Hispanic Arizona, 1536–1856.* Tucson: University of Arizona Press, 1987.

Sheridan, Thomas E. *Arizona: A History.* Tucson: University of Arizona Press, 1995.

Sheridan, Thomas E. and Nancy J. Parezo, eds. *Paths of Life: American Indians of the Southwest and Northern Mexico.* Tucson: University of Arizona Press, 1996.

Simmons, Marc. *New Mexico: A Bicentennial History.* New York: W.W. Norton, 1977.

Sonnichsen, C. L. *Tucson: The Life and Times of an American City.* Norman: University of Oklahoma Press, 1982.

Spicer, Edward. *Cycles of Conquest: The Impact of Spain, Mexico, and the United States on the Indians of the Southwest, 1533–1960.* Tucson: University of Arizona Press, 1962.

Sweeney, Edwin R. *Cochise: Chiricahua Apache Chief.* Norman: University of Oklahoma Press, 1991.

Thrapp, Dan L. *The Conquest of Apacheria.* Norman: University of Oklahoma Press, 1967.

Timmons, W. H. *El Paso: A Borderland History.* El Paso: Texas Western Press, 1990.

Utley, Robert M. *High Noon in Lincoln: Violence on the Western Frontier.* Albuquerque: University of New Mexico Press, 1987.

Weber, David J. *The Mexican Frontier, 1821–1846: The American Southwest Under Mexico.* Albuquerque: University of New Mexico Press, 1982.

——*The Spanish Frontier in North America.* New Haven: Yale University Press, 1992.

Westphall, Victor. *The Public Domain in New Mexico, 1854–1891.* Albuquerque: University of New Mexico Press, 1965.

Index

Photography Credits

Front cover: George H. Huey. Copyright page: George H. H. Huey. Contents: *Top to bottom*, George H. H. Huey, Marshall Trimble, Arizona Historical Society 20775, Michael Collier. 4: J. C. Leacock. 5: J. C. Leacock. 6: Corbis/Bettman. 7: George H. H. Huey. 8: William Stone. 9: Jack Dykinga. 10: Larry Ulrich. 12: David Muench. 13: *Top*, Courtesy of the California History Room, California State Library, Sacramento, California; *bottom*, George H. H. Huey. 14: *Top*, Denver Public Library, Western History Dept.; *bottom*, Arizona Historical Society 14224. 15: David Muench. 16: George H. H. Huey. 18: *Top*, Arizona Historical Society 69158; *bottom*, Jack Dykinga. 19: *Top*, Arizona State Museum, University of Arizona C-29811c; *bottom*, George H. H. Huey; *background*, Arthur Schott from *Report on the United States and Mexican Boundary Survey* by William H. Emory, 1857-1859. 20: C.S. Fly, courtesy of National Archives & Records Administration. 21: George H. H. Huey. 22: *Top*, courtesy Kit Carson Historic Museums; *bottom*, National Museum of the American Indian. 23: *Top*, Museum of New Mexico 22938, *bottom*, H. H. Cross, Kit Carson, 0126.1785, from the collection of Gilcrease Museum, Tulsa. 24: *Top*, courtesy of National Archives & Records Administration; *bottom*, courtesy Museum of New Mexico 15949. 25: Gene Balzer. 26: *Sibley* courtesy of Museum of New Mexico 50541; *revolvers* Marshall Trimble; *background*, Marshall Trimble; *Fort Union*, George H. H. Huey. 28: *Top*, Arizona Historical society 20957; *bottom*, Arizona Historical Society 25266. 29: Tom Bean. 30: Montana Historical Society, Helena, 946-434. 31: George H. H. Huey. 32: *Top*, Corbis/Bettman; *bottom*, Western History Collections, University of Oklahoma Libraries 2169. 33: Laurence Parent. 34: George H. H. Huey. 35: *Catron* courtesy of Museum of New Mexico 13309; *Eskiminzin*, National Archives & Records Administration, *background*, Arizona Historical Society 14839. 36: National Museum of the American Indian. 37: George H. H. Huey. 38: Arizona Historical Society 19775. 39: George H. H. Huey. 40-41: *Background*, Arizona Historical Society; *left to right*, Arizona Historical Society 25,638; Arizona Historical Society 1299; courtesey Museum of New Mexico 77022; National Museum of the American Indian; Arizona Historical Society 19705; Arizona Historical Society, 78165; Smithsonian, 2495-A; National Archives & Records Administration. 42: Arizona Historical Society 4267. 43: George H. H. Huey. 44: Michael Collier. 45: *Inset*, Jerome Historical Society; *background*, California State Railroad Museum. 46: *Top*, Denver Public Library, Western History Dept.; *bottom*, Library of Congress 80299. 47: George H. H. Huey. 48: Montana Historical Society, Helena. 50: George H. H. Huey. 51: *Inset*, Culver Pictures; *background*, courtesy Museum of New Mexico 5345. 52: Arizona Collection, Arizona State University Libraries. 53: Arizona Historical Society 20775. 54: *Top*, by Mark Dolce, Jerome Historical Society; *bottom*, Arizona Historical Society 24869. 55: George H. H. Huey. 56: *Earp brothers*, Buffalo Bill Historical Center, Cody, Wyo., Vincent Mercaldo Collection; *Clantons*, Western History Collections, University of Oklahoma Libraries; *Baby Pony*, Arizona Historical Society; *background*, Arizona Historical Society 44,688. 57: Arizona Historical Society 64,659. 58: Arizona Historical Society 59,415. 59: *Top*, Kansas State Historical Society, Topeka, Kansas; *inset*, Patrick Fischer; *background*, Chicago Historical Society. 60: *Top*, Arizona Historical Society 26719; *bottom*, Yuma Territorial Prison Records. 61: Tom Till. 62: Arizona State University Libraries. 63: *Inset*, Arizona Historical Society 58937; *background*, Arizona Historical Society 44111. 64: Heard Museum. 65: Larry Ulrich. 66: *Top*, Heard Museum, Fred Harvey Collection; *bottom*, Heard Museum, Fred Harvey Collection. 67: Adriel Heisey. 68: *Top*, Patrick Fischer; *bottom*, Heard Museum, Fred Harvey Collection. 69: *Top*, Heard Museum, Fred Harvey Collection; *bottom*, Gene Balzer. 70: *Top*, Larry Ulrich; *bottom*, Arizona Historical Society 90382; *background*, Bandelier National Monument. 71: George H. H. Huey. 72: *Top*, Jerome Historical Society; *bottom*, Tom Till. 73: Jack Dykinga. 74: Larry Ulrich. 75: Michael Collier/Condit. 76: Copyright 1997, Mark A. Culbertson. 77: J.C Leacock. Back Cover: George H. H. Huey.